Characteristics of a Great and Progressive Leader

& other

Quick Tips on Being a Great Leader

Norma J. Spivey

authorHOUSE®

AuthorHouse™
1663 Liberty Drive
Bloomington, IN 47403
www.authorhouse.com
Phone: 833-262-8899

This book is a work of non-fiction. Unless otherwise noted, the author and the publisher make no explicit guarantees as to the accuracy of the information contained in this book and in some cases, names of people and places have been altered to protect their privacy.

Published by AuthorHouse 02/15/2022

ISBN: 978-1-6655-4907-3 (sc)
ISBN: 978-1-6655-4912-7 (e)

Print information available on the last page.

Norma J. Spivey Illustrator

This book is printed on acid-free paper.

Contents

Dedications

- I want to dedicate this little book to my father, John. He always told his children "If I had as much education as y'all, I could do anything." He is also my inspiration for writing this book because he always talked about starting a business one day.

- I want to dedicate this book to my mother, Mary. She always told me, "Don't worry about the money, just make the grade," when I was in college.

- I want to dedicate this book to my daughter, Kimberlin. She kept on telling me "Momma, you are smart enough to figure out how to write the book by yourself."

- I want to dedicate this book to my siblings, John, Lee, Iris, and Roger. They have supported me in whatever I have decided to do in life.

- I want to dedicate this book to all the upper management, managers, supervisors, team leaders, and teachers. They have inspired me over the years to use my experience and their actions to write this little book to produce or assist people in becoming or continuing to be great leaders.

Introduction/About the Author

In this little book you will find valuable information from Norma Jean Spivey who has management experience and has observed, analyzed, critiqued, and monitored people in management positions. She has a bachelor's degree in Business Administration, which she chose to specialize in Human Resource Management. She has a master's degree in Elementary Education, and she will always continue to be certified to teach in the field.

Her time in the workforce has given her the opportunity to see managers, supervisors, and other leaders in many work environments. Her expertise and advice come from both white collar and blue collared working environments.

Norma has worked as a manager, supervisor, trainer, quality inspector, crew leader, educator, primary counselor, financial support worker, employment representative, insurance agent, choreographer, machine operator, and head cashier. In these positions she was able to see many characteristics and management styles of great leaders and those who needed much improvement. She is a JEAN of all trades.

This little book is not in chapters. The information is given in small sections. So, this setup will guarantee a quick read of valuable information that can be obtained in a very short length of time. She has also decided to use small sections, so that you could easily get back to certain sections that you feel will be beneficial to you.

If you are thinking seriously about making your time in a leadership position better and brighter in the future for those who you manage and for yourself, you have chosen the right little book. You should always remember as you read that it does not matter what race, color, creed, nationality, or gender that you may be a part of; you can work hard and become or continue to be a great and progressive leader.

We are going to begin by giving a definition of a manager/supervisor. A manager/supervisor is a person who is in charge, runs, or directs a department, business, etc. This is also a person who can be an overseer of a group, organization, or an operation.

One thing you should always think about is whether you really feel that you are the person that can be suitable for such a position. It's not always an easy job each day to be in a leadership position. You cannot just take the role because of the title and the money. If you do, it can become overwhelming. It will be this way because it is something you really did not have in your heart to do. You must be able and willing to multi-task. You will not succeed in this type of position if you approach your assignment with a lazy and laid-back attitude. The way any operation runs is a primary reflection of the people that are in charge.

Throughout the author's time as a regular employee, manager, supervisor, crew leader, etc., she ended up labeling or giving each leader a name that fitted their actions and behaviors. In the paragraphs ahead, you will find characteristics and tips that are pros and cons of anyone in a leadership position.

The New Leader

If you are new in a management position, do not try to start on the first day changing things around. Especially if you do not have a clue about how things really operate in the area that you are assigned to manage. You do not need to go in trying to micromanage your employees. You should at least take a few days to explore, research, observe, analyze, monitor and critique each area. You will be able to see exactly what you need to focus on after this process. Then, you can figure out whether any changes need to be made to help your department get or stay in tip top shape. If there is a safety issue of course, that will need your immediate attention. You must maintain a safe working environment.

The challenge of leadership is to be strong, but not rude; be kind, but not weak; be bold, but not bully; be thoughtful, but not lazy; be humble, but not timid; be proud, but not arrogant; have humour, but without folly. – *Jim Rohn, American motivational speaker*

The Communicator

You should always communicate with your employees. Poor communication always causes an operation to run poorly. People usually get frustrated when they have not been informed or misinformed of important events or situations. If a manager does not implement a good line of communication, it will ALWAYS have a negative effect on the employees and the customers as well. Always Inform your crew of changes and updates about every situation in the company. If you do not have enough time to communicate the information verbally, please make sure you communicate the information in writing. Always try to have the employees' signatures on important information. By following this process, it will help the manager keep an accurate record of what the management and their employees have discussed. Everyone should know what they need to have knowledge of in the facility. Managers should constantly reiterate and follow up on the rules and goals of their business.

The art of communication is the language of leadership.

-James Humes, American speechwriter

The Team Player

You should always be willing to help your employees. Someone coined the phrase "There is no 'I' in team." Everyone must work together. You should always be willing to take the initiative and help your employees and co-workers. Whether you're in a crisis such as being short of help, need to increase production rapidly, or not. Your crew and co-workers should be able to see whether you will willingly help them with no problem. They need to see that you will support them in completing any task. After all, how can you be a good leader and not know how to do the jobs of the people that are under your supervision. It is very important that they see that you do not think that you are too good to complete any task. You should never ask someone to do a job that you would never be willing to do. Plus, it's not like you must do their job every day. A good leader should always be ready to stand up and give a helping hand.

"Coming together is a beginning. Keeping together is progress. Working together is success." *--Henry Ford, American industrialist*

The Empathizer

You should never forget that your employees are human and not robots. All of us have feelings. Every day is not going to be a perfectly good day. We know that life can bring you situations that are expected and unexpected. Some are good, and some are not so good.

So, when a problem arises for one of your members, please take a humanly approach to resolve or suggest different solutions that can make things better. We know that every problem will not be eliminated, but you should work hard at making the right decisions to make a person's day run smoother. No one is asking you to be a counselor, but you show your employees that you do have some concerns for whatever they may be experiencing at certain times.

When it comes to employees applying for other jobs within the company, do not hold them back. It is recommended that you should always have aces in place in each position, but do not be selfish and keep them in a position that an employee has obviously outgrown. You can have that exceptional employee train the next employee to be just as efficient as they were in that position. You do not want the employee to be dissatisfied and frustrated to the point that they seek other employment. Then, you will have a good employee transferring their great skills to some other company. You should want your best employees with great potential to be even more beneficial to the company.

"If there is any one secret of success, it lies in the ability to get the other person's point of view and see things from that person's angle as well as from your own." *-Henry Ford, American industrialist*

The Arrogant Leader

When a manager has an arrogant attitude, this behavior can easily become a problem. It can almost automatically cause a negative feeling to develop between a manager and their employees. This behavior can cause employees to perform poorly or pursue another job. Always keep in mind that no one knows everything. You should always be open for suggestions to make things run smoothly. If an employee wants to give some feedback about a situation, you should always listen whether you take their advice or not. If someone has a better remedy than what you can possibly put in place, do not ever deny them the credit. Anyone can have great ideas even if they are not in a leadership position.

"By my count, more business leaders have failed and derailed because of arrogance than any other character flaw." - *Harvey Mackay, American businessman and journalist*

The Threat Maker

You should never constantly threaten your employees. No one wants to hear someone threatening them every time something goes wrong. Everyone wants to be treated with respect and not be treated as if they are a little child and not an adult. No one wants to constantly hear, "I am going to write you up!!! "I am going to give you a reprimand!!!"

By threatening someone, they may not put forth any effort to do a good job. Several threats may make them feel that they are going to eventually lose their job and possibly sooner than later. It will have your employees uncomfortable and tense when trying to perform their jobs. If you are having some type of issue with a certain individual, please do not blame everyone for the problem. No one wants to hear that they are doing a bad job when the situation has nothing to do with them. Constant threats can bring your team's morale down in any work environment. Constant threats can also be considered as forms of bullying, harassment, and micromanaging. In any workplace, there should be zero tolerance for all these issues.

Those that are the loudest in their threats are the weakest in their actions. - *Charles Caleb Colton, British priest and writer*

The Complainer

You should never continuously complain about the type of day or issue that may arise. Always give positive feedback and statements even when your surroundings are nearly in shambles or completely disorganized. You need to be the cheerleader who always says that things will get better. You should immediately start searching for solutions that can change the atmosphere. Always remember that you can have the advantage of setting the tone of how the night or day will be on a shift.

"What you're supposed to do when you don't like a thing is change it. If you can't change it, change the way you think about it. Don't complain."-*Maya Angelou, American poet and author*

The Procrastinator

As a manager, never constantly put things off that needs to be done. You should perform each task as quickly as possible. You do not want your duties to turn into or have a snowball effect. Tasks are always rolling in and you do not want your stack of duties to get larger. You do not want to become overwhelmed to the point that nothing really gets done. Everything can become chaotic and unorganized if you do not prioritize. The people who work for you can possibly become frustrated and tempers may flare up also. If you do not procrastinate, your operation can run much more smoothly than you think is possible. In return, you will also be able to retain more employees with positive attitudes.

"You may delay, but time will not, and lost time is never found again." — *Benjamin Franklin*

"My advice is to never do tomorrow what you can do today. Procrastination is the thief of time."– *Charles Dickens, English writer and social critic*

The Blame Shifter

Whenever you have made mistakes and the outcome of a situation or project did not turn out right, **DO NOT** blame others. Especially if the decision was made directly by you. You will be respected more for owning up to your mistakes. It happens!!! Every decision might not be the right one, but at least be able to say that you made the best one according to your knowledge about the situation that was at hand.

Sometimes, people are not around to defend themselves and they do not need to be put in an uncomfortable predicament. If you make a mistake, you should be ready to quickly come up with a solution to correct the problem.

Great leaders don't rush to blame. They instinctively look for solutions. -*Nina Easton, American journalist and author*

The Virtual Leader

When working remotely, you want to have the workplace as traditional as possible. What does this mean? It means that your daily, weekly, monthly, and yearly tasks and activities should go on as if you were in a brick-and-mortar work environment. Your performance and those who work for you should not go slacking and lacking. You still need to be a team player even though you are virtual. The following items are necessary, and they are key focus areas for you to incorporate in your remote/virtual work environment. You will be able to have much success in achieving your goals in your organization.

- Find out the **computer savviness** of your team. This information will be helpful if you are having technical difficulties with your computer and especially if your department has a deadline to submit a project. One of your crew members may need to represent the department by submitting information on your behalf.

- You and your team members should always be willing to **upgrade your computer skills.** Technology is always updating. You should make sure you are parallel with its updates.

- **Create a checklist** for each person in your department. If they have tasks that need to be completed daily, you can have them submit short tasks daily or by the end of the week with samples of their work.

- Since you **mostly communicate in writing,** always make sure your response is written appropriately. You should not use all caps when writing messages and responses, unless you have informed the employees within the organization that it reflects something of high importance. All caps have been known to be and can be a form of yelling.

- Always be willing to **lend a helping hand** to those who may be struggling as they are working online and possibly having their first-time experience in doing so.

- Always have a **meeting with your team** even if it only lasts 10 or 15 minutes. You may want to give a major progress report to influence and motivate everyone to keep up the good work. You can use it for a check in or for attendance; whatever you choose to call it. The meeting can also be to make sure everyone is on the same page on knowing what is expected for the project in progress.

- When it comes to **time zones**, you should make sure you know the time zones of each team member. Always plan meetings, workshops, and other activities at times that will work for everyone. If it is not possible, record the meeting so that the ones who were not in attendance can know what was discussed in the meeting.

- You should create a brief survey and have your team members **complete the survey** at the end of the month. You will be able to receive feedback about how they are feeling about their position, work, projects, etc.

- A great virtual leader should be able to **give a quarterly and honest evaluation** for each team member. Everyone needs to know if they are really doing a great job or there is still room for improvement. You should create and **give an employee of the month award** for the employee that is doing an exceptional job or to the one who has improved the most.

Upper-Level Management

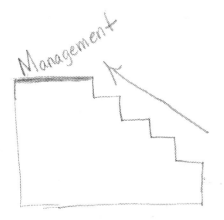

When it comes to upper management, you should always work hard at not being known by title only. It does not hurt to come out into the heart of the business to see what is really going on. You should want to know the people who are directly involved in providing the good product, products, service, and/or services for your business. The people that are at the base and fundamentally in charge of your business are important. They are the little people that are really in the driver's seat. They are the ones you want to influence and satisfy; so that they will take pride in their work. Even though you are the one who delegate the duties that come down through the chain of command, they are the ones who keep the paychecks and bonuses coming for you and themselves. You should always show respect and give support to the little guys on the totem pole.

Management's job is to convey leadership's message in a compelling and inspiring way. Not just in meetings, but also by example.
-Jeffrey Gitomer, American author

Additional Dos and Don'ts and Quick Tips for Great Leadership

Favoritism

Favoritism is a major NO-NO. You should never do this because it can cause hostility in the workplace. You should never consider yourself as part of a clique, clan, or posse that you hang out with when you are trying to lead people. You want to always remain neutral in the treatment of your employees. When favoritism is shown, there is no guarantee that all the employees will do the best job that they can possibly do. It is hard and uncomfortable when you delegate duties that are not well liked by the people that are your buddies and so-called friends. The author is not saying that you should not be cordial and polite to everyone, but do not over do it because in the end you might lose that status of being a good and professional leader. You are not in the workplace to make friends. You are at work to accomplish goals and tasks that will make your company run successfully. They may say that there is no reason to give our best performance because Linda or Steve will get the recognition. You do not want your crew to be holding any resentment toward you and other employees.

Leaders who practice favoritism in the workplace have no chance to build a culture of trust. *-Robert Whipple, American actor*

Employee Hiring and Retention

When it comes to maintaining a full staff/crew, always remember the following regulations to increase the amount of time people will stay on the job.

- Stay organized, alert, and focused as much as possible
- Follow the rules the same for each employee
- Consistently check to make sure you are fully staffed

- Properly train each employee

- Implement some type of mentoring program

- Receive and listen to feedback from every employee

- Create and implement ideas that produce a comfortable work environment

When it comes to hiring, it can be better if you hire within the company. The people that should be chosen are the ones that have a good track record of getting a job done and the ones who have a good work ethic. Some companies prefer to go outside the company to hire management because they can get prospects that are experienced. The experience that they bring to the job may not necessarily be the experience you are looking for in a leader.

If you hire within, the people are already familiar with the company and they could already know more than you think they know about how your company operates on a day to day basis. They are in the mix every day. Then, you won't need as much training for positions. In addition to less training, you will be able to retain more employees because they already know the ups and downs of how a day in the business can possibly shape up. You can also train them exactly how you want them because they will not be coming in injecting another company's bad ideas if they had a bad experience at their former company.

Newcomers may be willing to learn to do the same things, but it would require more training. You will need to teach them the basics plus additional material that a present employee already knows. The cost, training, and time management will just be overall cheaper for the company in the long run if you hire within.

"Retention is best when the learner is involved." - *Edward Scannell, American author and human resources expert*

Training

Every organization should have a formal training program. When it comes to training, a business will benefit more if it has a set of people who are specifically chosen to focus only or mostly on getting the employees fully and accurately trained. It is important that you are thoroughly and properly trained as a leader. You should always be willing to seek and receive extra training that will be beneficial for your employees and yourself. When it comes to training your employees, always do the best job as possible. If you do not thoroughly train them, you will end up retraining more than you would care to do so. Even if you assign someone else to do the training, always follow up on the person that has been trained. You might be able to add something extra and/ or clarify information that has been given to the trainee. It is important for you to know how much information has been obtained and retained by every individual.

As you train the employee, make them as comfortable as possible. They should not feel intimidated by the trainer. The trainer should put them at ease. For example, they can do a little small talk by saying something like, "Have you ever worked in a manufacturing plant before? "It's a nice day out there today."

Always put your aces in place in your organization, but make sure everyone is trained properly. You should never train people for just one position. Cross-training is a must and a plus for any operation. It may take some extra time to train each employee in other positions, but it will really pay off and be positively worth it in the long run. You should not have to depend on just one person to perform a duty. Each employee should be allowed to become comfortable in other positions and not just in their primary position. When you can change around positions, most people will do a better job because they are not feeling overwhelmed by doing the same job. They will be able to catch a break from mostly doing what they may consider as tedious work. Always train your employees to never be wasteful. You should think about ways to save whether you are selling a product or delivering a service to your clients and customers. When it comes to your training program, always remember the following key factors:

- **T**ake the time to train
- **R**etrain your employees periodically
- **A**sk questions to see if your people know key information

- **I**mplement new ideas to make jobs run smoother continuously

- **N**ever do a rush job, train people thoroughly

If it is possible, assign a mentor to each crew, associate, or staff member. It is necessary to have a mentor that has a good reputation of doing a good job when it comes to their assignments and duties. They should be hard-working, dependable, and a team player. A mentorship can be considered as a part of your training needs and can assist in retaining employees.

"It's all to do with the training: you can do a lot if you're properly trained." - *Elizabeth II, Queen of Great Britain*

Scheduling

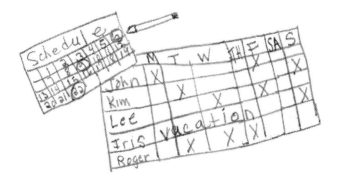

If you are a leader in the retail or restaurant industry, when it comes to scheduling, **<u>DO NOT</u>** schedule the same people every weekend. You should always rotate the weekends. Nobody wants to work every weekend. If you do rotate, people will have less of an attitude when they work because they know that they will be off the following weekend. You will see that you will be able to retain more employees. The turnover will not be at a high rate. Everyone wants to be able to spend time with family and friends. It cannot be reiterated enough. It is very important that you take a little more extra time to make the employee schedule.

In modern life, we tend to forget family values because of the hectic schedule. – *Mahesh Babu, Indian Actor*

Confidentiality

If an employee decides to confide in you about a personal situation, you should keep it confidential. It's not something that you should go out and tell their fellow co-workers. You should show your employees that you can be honest and trustworthy. You can let them know that you are concerned about their well- being. Especially, if you can see that there is something not quite right about them at the beginning, during, and after work. You don't have to be a full fledge counselor, but it does not hurt to be there to give a helping hand or ear every now and then if possible.

Confidentiality is a virtue of the loyal, as loyalty is the virtue of faithfulness. -*Edwin Louis Cole, American Author*

Goal Setting

You should always have a game plan on how you want to get things done. When setting goals, you make sure that they are doable for your crew and for yourself. Always make sure that when you delegate a task, that it is specific in details. You must give enough time for the duty to be done. It should be a reasonable time for results to be seen. You should make sure it is totally related to a situation that can make everything run smoothly and correctly in the business.

People with clear, written goals accomplish far more in a short period of time than people without them could ever imagine- *Brian Tracy, American motivational speaker and writer*

Journaling

You should always write in a journal, at the end of your shift whether you work days or nights. Each entry can and should implement a process to follow to get things done. When journaling, make sure you write down how the process progressed throughout your shift. Then, you can evaluate the process by making a list or note about the pros and cons on how your time began and ended. This task will help you think about how you could have tackled or approached situations differently if they were solved without a good outcome. You should always try to have more than one solution to a problem.

I journal at the end of every day and just keep track of how things are going. - *Betsy Hodges, American Politician*

Problem Solving

You should not push a problem to the back burner. If possible, discuss it immediately or if not, you should discuss the issue as soon as you can find an appropriate time. If you do not, it can escalate into a much bigger problem. You never want to allow a situation to get completely out of control. It will not be good if it accumulates and have a snowball effect. You could be asked at any time the questions, "What did you do to eliminate the problem?" "What steps are you following to correct the issue?"

When it comes to a solution, work hard at finding every possible resolution. You should always try to choose an answer that is best for the business and everyone involved.

Most people spend more time and energy going around problems than in trying to solve them. *– Henry Ford, American industrialist*

Awards

Every business should have some types of awards for being an exceptional employee. The awards should be separate when they are given. This means that there should be a set of awards for management and a set for regular employees. When the awards are together, it does not look good that a member of upper management won the cash award over the regular employees. You should try to be creative at developing something a little extra for a job well done, even if you are a department manager. It does not have to be something costly. It can be something as little as showing recognition to an employee each month and giving them a gift card or a free lunch meal. When it comes to an employee work performance, never forget to let them know that they are doing a good job. It does not matter how old a person can become; they still do not mind receiving a little praise and recognition. Even if you choose to just tell them verbally, the words can go a long way. Everyone wants to be appreciated.

The way to develop the best that is in a person is by appreciation and encouragement. -*Charles Schwab, American investor, financial executive, and philanthropist*

Awards can give you a tremendous amount of encouragement to keep getting better, no matter how young or old you are. – *Alan Alda, actor, author, activist, director, screenwriter, comedian*

Social Media

Although Social Media can be good for marketing your business, it is important that you communicate with your employees about the potential dangers that can possibly occur with Social Media (Facebook, Twitter, Instagram, etc.). It can create a hostile environment for the workplace. If it is not used in a respectful and mature manner, it could possibly cause someone to be terminated or harmed in some way. Always encourage them to say something nice about someone or just say nothing at all.

If it is used properly, they can avoid chaos and confusion. You should let the employees know that they can be monitored at any time.

Social media is not the place to work out your problems with people. - *Lewis Howes, American author, entrepreneur, and former professional arena league football player*

Safety

Unfortunately, there has been an increase in violence around the world in white-collar and blue-collar workplace environments. In a leadership position, you should always discuss safety as a company and within different departments. Employees should be encouraged to speak up about anything that looks or sounds strange or suspicious. You should always have a game plan for you and your employees to follow in any awkward, uncomfortable, or hostile situation. Everyone should always stay alert. In any work environment, make sure you pay close attention to your surroundings.

If your business use radios/walkie talkies, you should always include them in your safety procedures and plans. You should communicate with the employees about using them in case of emergencies or any other incident that requires immediate attention to protect your co-workers and other employees. If your business invests in these devices, it increases the chances for the employees to know first - hand about what is going on in the workplace. Even if they are not physically at the place when or where very important information is stated and given.

When an employee uses a radio to notify everyone that there is danger in the workplace, they can make these example statements listed below:

- White male, white shirt has entered back exit with gun.
- Black male, green shirt, with gun is in the front office.
- Asian female, red t-shirt on main aisle with knife.
- Safety mode, I repeat safety mode

These statements are once again statements that can be used to protect your facility. You will need to choose or create statements that would be appropriate for your facility's atmosphere and architectural design.

Everyone should be concerned about their fellow co-workers and themselves. You should always be willing to be cordial and respectful to and toward one another. You can never reiterate your safety rules and regulation too much. Safety should always be first and a priority in every workplace. The following video is additional information that can be shown to employees on how to **RUN, HIDE, and FIGHT** when there has been an intruder entering the workplace.

In 2011, the Texas State Office of Risk Management produced an Active Shooter Emergency Preparedness video. In the video, office employees are being advised on how to address an active shooter. This video can be useful in any workplace environment.

https://youtu.be/w9nldEZvl6k

Safety is a common denominator across all aspects of life, hence knowledge should always be shared. It is not a matter for industry it is a matter for humanity.

- Doug Bourne, Australian Rules Footballer

Intimidation, harassment, and violence have no place in democracy-*Mo Ibrahim, Sudanese-British entrepreneur and philanthropist*

Balance Work and Play

I don't want you to get me wrong, but when you're a manager, it is not always an easy task. A person must be able to be more organized than not. Organization is a key factor in how to balance your life in a way so that you won't start hating your job. Do not be afraid to delegate some duties and make sure you follow up on how the delegated duties are shaping up. You will be able to spend more quality time with your family and yourself if you manage your time wisely.

When it comes to managing your own time, it is recommended that you invest in a desktop calendar and a writing journal. You can also keep notes on your electronic devices such as a computer, tablet or cell phone. These items will help you stay on track. When you use a calendar, a journal, and an electronic device of your choosing, they can help you keep up with your number one priority on a daily, weekly, and monthly basis. They will also help you to leave your work at work and not have you focusing on job-related issues outside of work.

Live and work but do not forget to play, to have fun in life and really enjoy it. -*Eileen Caddy, English Celebrity*

Conclusion

When you're on any job, you must know that positions and duties may change. Are you the person that needs to be promoted to the next level? If so, the already proven tips in this book will make you a better manager, supervisor or team Leader for others and yourself in any work environment. You know that no one is perfect, but you should always do your best when you are in a leadership position. The author feels that the number one characteristic of being a great leader is being a team player. Don't be afraid to jump in and help your team when times get hard. Several people have often said and say that we are not on the job to make friends, but we should not be on the job to make enemies either. No one will turn down a helping hand. Everyone can benefit from receiving the extra help especially when it comes from the one who is in charge.

Always **BE PROFESSIONAL**!!! No one can ever emphasize this statement enough. If you do not know how, you should fake it until you make it by using these great tips. The website at the end of this book is also a very helpful site in helping you to become a professional leader.

Throughout your time in a leading role, always remember the statements below:

-You should always remember that it does not matter what race, color, creed, nationality, or gender that you may be a part of, you can work hard and be or become a better and progressive leader.

- Always remember the golden rule is to treat others the way you want to be treated.

"Always treat your employees exactly as you want them to treat your best customers."
--Stephen R. Covey, author of The Seven Habits of Highly Effective People

"To win in the marketplace you must first win in the workplace."

--Doug Conant, Fmr. President and CEO of the Campbell Soup Company

The Differences Between a Boss and a Leader

Boss	Leader
Demands	Coaches
Relies on Authority	Relies on Goodwill
Issues Ultimatums	Generates Enthusiasm
Says "I"	Says "We"
Uses People	Develops People
Takes Credit	Gives Credit
Places the Blame	Accepts Blame
Says "Go"	Says "Let's Go
My way is the only way	Strength in Unity

Questions for Leaders and Possible Leaders

1. Am I really management material?

2. Am I willing to go the extra mile to make sure things are running smoothly?

3. Am I willing to be a team player?

4. Am I a good communicator?

5. What kind of impact will the leadership role have on my co-workers/ personal/family life?

6. Am I taking the position to support the company or just for money only?

7. What did I learn from reading this book?

Tips that are Identified
and Beneficial to You

1. What did you learn from these tips that you had not previously thought about?

2. Which of these tips will you start focusing on immediately?

3. Which tip do you have the most issues with performing?

4. What tip do you feel a co-worker needs to work on?

5. Which tip are you a master at performing?

Credits

Share, Jacob "*11 Ways to Be a Professional at Work*" 25 August 2018 Retrieved from https://www.livecareer. com/career/advice/jobs/professionalism

The State of Risk Management-sorm.state.tx.us. (2016, Feb. 26) "*How to Survive an Active Shooter*" [online video clip] *YouTube.* YouTube 2 July 2018 Retrieved from https://youtu.be/w9nldEZvl6k

Wolfe, David The Difference Between a Boss and a Leader, Facebook (2016, March 23)

Printed in the United States
by Baker & Taylor Publisher Services